D1454733

ISBN 1-58660-645-X

Previously published as *Favorite Family Holiday Activities.*

All Scripture quotations are taken from the King James Version of the Bible.

Published by Humble Creek, P.O. Box 719, Uhrichsville, Ohio 44683

Printed in China.
5 4 3 2 1

family activities for the holidays

Ellyn Sanna

Making Christmas Memories

Christmas is a special time—a time of excitement, wonder, and love. As adults, however, too often we allow our Christmas joy to be dimmed by the weight of holiday chores and long shopping lists; we let the hassle of holiday crowds cloud our hearts with impatience; and we forget about the quiet wonder of a newborn Baby.

This book has some suggestions for ways you and your family can recapture your sense of Christmas joy. Don't try to do all of the activities (or you'll end up more hassled and stressed than ever), but pick and choose those that especially speak to you. Most of all, these activities are designed to include the whole family. Christmas is a time to share our love, making special memories to last a lifetime.

Behold, a virgin shall be with child,
and shall bring forth a son,
and they shall call his name Emmanuel,
which being interpreted is,
God with us.

MATTHEW 1:23

Nativity Scenes

Put a nativity scene under your Christmas tree—or on the mantel or the top of a bookshelf. Try to find one that is not too fragile or valuable. Spend time with your children talking about it. Encourage them to interact with it using their imaginations.

Christmas Picture Book

Make a Christmas card book for your young children—or have your older children make books that can be shared with a preschool class or young Sunday school class. Erase or remove the signatures on four old Christmas cards and open them out flat. Stack the cards on top of each other in the same direction so that all the pictures are facing down on the same side. Sew the cards together along the crease and refold to form the book. Press the cards with a heavy book if necessary to make them lie flat.

MATERIALS

old Christmas cards

needle and thread

Handprint Cards

A unique way to share your family's Christmas wishes with friends is with a special handmade card. First, have the father use a colored pencil to trace around his hand on a sheet of paper. Next, have the mother trace her hand inside the outline of her husband's. Then trace around the children's hands, each inside the outlines of the others. Use different colors for each person. Add Christmas greetings to complete your distinctively personalized card.

MATERIALS

paper

colored markers

Advent Wreath

Make an Advent wreath with your family. Fasten four candle-holders into an evergreen wreath. Drill holes into a board or set holders into a plaster of paris mold to make sure they are secure. Cover the base with damp sand to keep the evergreen branches fresh longer. The traditional colors for the candles are three purple and one rose (to be used on the third Sunday). Some people, however, like to use all red candles, or all white, or all purple. Light one candle on the first Sunday in Advent and another each Sunday until all the candles are lit. Make this a special time of prayer and song.

Materials

- four candles
- board or plaster of paris
- evergreen branches
- sand

Love Box

Create a Love Box and keep it throughout the year. All year, collect items in the box that could be used as gifts at Christmastime. Encourage your children to make their own additions to the box (for example, their "Happy Meal" toys). When Christmas comes, the items in this box can provide gifts for families in your community, even those you don't know well. Another possible use for the Love Box is to collect in it things to give to a specific ministry or mission.

And she brought forth her firstborn son,
and wrapped him in swaddling clothes,
and laid him in a manger;
because there was no room for them in the inn.

LUKE 2:7

Intangible Gifts

Teach your children that gifts don't have to be material things. Have them make ornaments from construction paper, cutting the paper in the shape of a stocking or an old-fashioned shoe. Cut out two of each form and have the child glue all the edges together except the top. Fasten a ribbon to the top corner in order to hang the ornament from the tree. The real gift, however, is a folded piece of paper inside the ornament on which the child writes a promise of something he or she will do for someone—for brother or sister, mother or father. In this way he or she learns that gifts of time are also legitimate gifts.

Materials

- colored construction paper
- glue
- ribbon
- paper and pen

Christmas Drives

Take a drive to see the Christmas lights. Bundle the kids into warm pajamas and blankets and tuck them into the car. Go out late at night so few other cars will be on the road and drive around slowly to see as many lights and decorations as you can. You might want to sing carols as you go.

"The Nutcracker"

Take your children to see "The Nutcracker Suite." They will be delighted by this Christmas ballet.

It came upon the midnight clear,
That glorious song of old,
From angels bending near the earth,
To touch their harps of gold:
"Peace on the earth, good will to men,
From heaven's all-gracious King."
The world in solemn stillness lay
To hear the angels sing.

EDMOND HAMILTON SEARS, 1834

Piñata

This is a Mexican tradition, which is part of the Christmas celebration. The piñata is filled with candy and small presents and is hung from the ceiling. Children are blindfolded, spun around, and given three tries to break open the piñata with a broom handle.

MATERIALS

- round balloon, inflated
- flowerpot
- water
- acrylic paint
- white glue
- petroleum jelly
- 1 cup flour
- newspaper
- colored tissue paper
- ribbons, two inches wide

Piñata Directions:

Rub a thin coating of petroleum jelly over the balloon and balance balloon, tied end down, in the flowerpot. Mix water slowly with the flour until paste is the consistency of pancake batter. Tear newspaper into two-inch strips and immerse strips in paste. Cover the balloon with the newspaper strips until all but the end in the flowerpot is covered.

Add two more layers of newspaper and let dry completely (about twenty-four hours). Pop the balloon and wipe out any excess petroleum jelly, then dry another twenty-four hours. Paint the piñata with acrylic paint and glue ribbons and tissue paper streamers to the bottom. Use an awl to punch three holes in the rim of the piñata and run strings through the holes for hanging.

The shepherds said one to another,
Let us now go even unto Bethlehem,
and see this thing which is come to pass,
which the Lord hath made known unto us.
And they came with haste, and found Mary,
and Joseph, and the babe lying in a manger.

LUKE 2:15–16

Story Time

Collect Christmas storybooks. Get as many different kinds as you can—books about the Christmas story, *Frosty the Snowman*, *The Christmas Carol.* During the Christmas season, read them to your children at bedtime.

Christmas Hospitality

Have a progressive dinner for families. This saves you and your friends from each having to host a separate meal. Start at one house for appetizers, move on to another for soup and salad, then to another for the main course, and end at the last house for coffee and dessert.

Time Capsule

At your family gathering, put together a time capsule to be opened in five years or more. In a waterproof container, put the front page of that day's newspaper and a list of everyone present (or a Polaroid picture of everyone). Get everyone to write down a wish and a prediction to add to the capsule. Add whatever other items you think of, such as children's drawings, jewelry, or an audiotape. Bury it in the attic or the garage to be opened on the Christmas of the year you've chosen.

Joy to the world! The Lord is come;
Let earth receive her King;
Let every heart prepare Him room,
And heaven and nature sing.

ISAAC WATTS, 1719

Sharing the Joy

Help out an elderly neighbor. Help him decorate his home, and fill his refrigerator for him. Drive him to Christmas services if he desires.

Hospital Cheer

Bring decorated baskets of Christmas treats to hospital patients, especially those who won't be able to spend Christmas with their families. Make sure your children help you pack and decorate the baskets.

MATERIALS

small wicker baskets
(can usually be bought cheaply from a craft store)

Christmas ribbons
candy
scented lotion
fresh fruits
magazines
paperback books

In the beginning was the Word,
and the Word was with God,
and the Word was God.
The same was in the beginning with God.
All things were made by him;
and without him was not any thing
made that was made.
In him was life; and the life was the light of men.
And the light shineth in darkness;
and the darkness comprehended it not.

JOHN 1:1–5

Use Your Organizational Skills

Help start a canned food drive at your church or a toy drive with your local police or fire department. Another idea is a coat and blanket drive to help homeless or needy people.

Christmas Newsletter

Send a family newsletter along with your Christmas cards. Write about your family's activities and achievements from throughout the past year. Older children can write their own stories; younger ones can dictate to you what they want to share. Add black and white photographs, artwork, and designs. If you don't have a computer capable of handling the graphics, go to a copy shop to have copies made.

A Gift a Day

Make an Advent calendar. Start with December 1 and continue through Christmas Eve or Christmas Day. Place a little gift for each member of the family in a bag under each date. Or you might want to write a special message or a Bible verse. Use your own ideas to make your Advent calendar unique.

Homemade Wrapping Paper

Instead of buying wrapping paper, use brown paper bags to make your own. You and your children can decorate the paper with paint, markers, or rubber stamps. Another idea is to wrap gifts in sheets of comics from the newspaper.

MATERIALS

- brown paper bags
- markers, crayons, or tempera paint
- scissors
- stamps and stamp pads

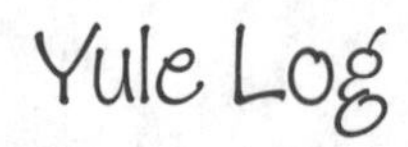

Get a log that has been split down the center, then smooth off the flat edge so that it will sit on a table without wobbling. Using a drill, make two or three holes in the rounded side, big enough to use as candle holders. Decorate the log with ribbons and pinecones and use it as a centerpiece. If you have a fireplace, on Christmas Day you might want to burn your log. Traditionally, each family member writes down the things he or she is sorry for doing over the past year. These are shared among the family, and then one by one the pieces of paper are burned in the Yule fire, symbolizing the total forgiveness we have in Christ.

Materials

- twelve- to eighteen-inch log, split in half
- pinecones
- drill
- ribbons
- candles

Candles

Make candles—for gifts or for your family's Christmas use. Use juice cans or milk cartons for molds and cord for wicks. Melt paraffin, then add stearic acid or beeswax before pouring the wax into the molds. Color can be added with your children's old crayons. Encourage your children to think of decorations to press into the outsides of the candles—buttons, pebbles, shells, dried flowers, etc.

Materials

- paraffin
- old crayons
- assorted hard objects (pretty stones, shells, etc.)
- stearic acid or beeswax
- juice cans or milk cartons

Joy to the earth! The Savior reigns;
Let men their songs employ;
While fields and floods, rocks, hills and plains
Repeat the sounding joy.

ISAAC WATTS, 1719

Unique Decorations

Buy clear glass Christmas balls and have family members decorate them with acrylic paint. Use makeup brushes or cotton swabs to apply the paint. Make sure everyone signs their artwork.

Materials

- clear glass Christmas balls
- makeup brushes or cotton swabs
- gold acrylic paint

Christmas Treasure Hunt

On Christmas Eve, set up a treasure hunt for your children, leading to a present. Give easy clues for the younger ones and make the clues a little more difficult for older children. Leave a candy cane or cookie beside some of the clues.

Christmas is a time for families, a time for being with children, a time for fun and merriment. Thank God for the special gift of our families! As busy grown-ups, we need to remember that all our activities—at Christmastime and all year round—should center on sharing the love of Christ with those around us. Even the simplest activities can become a heritage of love, stored up in our children's memories for them to share one day with their own families.

What I'd like to have for Christmas
I can tell you in a minute.
The family all around me,
And the home with laughter in it.

EDGAR A. GUEST